Making the Grade

.

HOW TO PASS YOUR MUSIC EXAM

Paul Harris

With a Foreword by
Evelyn Barbirolli

Music Department
OXFORD UNIVERSITY PRESS
Oxford and New York

Oxford University Press, Walton Street, Oxford OX2 6DP

Oxford New York Toronto
Delhi Bombay Calcutta Madras Karachi
Petaling Jaya Singapore Hong Kong Tokyo
Nairobi Dar es Salaam Cape Town
Melbourne Auckland

and associated companies in
Berlin Ibadan

Oxford is a trade mark of Oxford University Press

British Library Cataloguing in Publication Data
Harris, Paul
    Making the grade.—(How to pass your music exam).
    1. Great Britain. Music. Examinations. Techniques
    I. Title   II. Series
    780.76
    ISBN 0–19–321348–6

Typeset by Rowland Phototypesetting Ltd
Printed in Great Britain by St Edmundsbury Press Ltd, Bury St Edmunds, Suffolk

Contents

Foreword

There are professional musicians who disapprove of exams, and more particularly of the competitions which may follow at a later stage. I am not of this opinion, but even if I were, I would have to accept that exams are part of musical life today.

Making the Grade is an excellent book, full of common sense and understanding. It will help you to keep your exam-taking in proportion, to work well, and, hopefully, with enjoyment! This book should be of the greatest possible value to those who are going to take an exam and to those teaching them to do so.

Among the many pieces of good advice given by Paul Harris is the suggestion that you read—and thoroughly digest!—sections of this book at a time, rather than try to go through the whole at one sitting. I would emphasize that you should begin with Chapter 1 and really pay particular attention to it before going any further.

Evelyn Barbirolli

Introduction

If you're preparing for a music exam, this is the handbook for you! The advice and guidance it gives will help make your preparation thorough and methodical, so that when you finally come to take the exam you'll really feel both ready and able to give your best.

This book is written for players of all instruments and for singers, but to avoid repetition 'instrumentalist' has been used to refer to players of instruments other than the piano. Most of the information is applicable whatever your instrument (or voice). Occasionally, where more specific guidance is necessary, the information is divided into particular sections, usually for keyboard players, string players (including guitarists), woodwind and brass players, percussionists, and singers.

Take pride in the way you prepare for an exam, and GOOD LUCK!

> You don't need to read this book all through at one sitting—pick out the sections that you're particularly concerned about or are working on at the time, and keep coming back and re-reading them until the ideas and methods really sink in.

1. Why take exams?

Music gives enormous pleasure to everyone. Actually performing it is a deeply enjoyable experience, whether your ambition is to accompany Christmas carols, play in your school or youth orchestra, sing in your local choir, appear at the Royal Festival Hall, or just play for pleasure at home. But to achieve success at any level, you'll need to develop a combination of *skill* and *musicianship*.

The particular skills needed to play or sing well are really quite complicated, and, as you well know, will only improve with a lot of practice. Eventually, with the help of a good teacher, a sense of commitment, and (probably most important) HARD WORK you *will* achieve them.

Musicianship (or *artistry*) is much more difficult to describe in words. It's to do with being able to play expressively and to give shape and character to your performances. Go to concerts, listen and watch carefully, and you'll begin to understand what artistry is all about. As a musician you are trying to express something very special. Some famous words by the great composer Richard Wagner may help give some idea:

Music is the speech of the heart.

So, having decided to learn a musical instrument, why bother to take exams? If you use the exam system carefully it should

- help to guide and direct your study
- help to develop your instrumental or vocal skills
- stimulate artistry
- act as a source of motivation
- encourage and monitor steady progress.

But be careful: don't allow exams to dictate your work and choice of repertoire to the exclusion of everything else. Having been through the full sequence of exams, you could find that you've learnt only a handful of pieces, perhaps never a complete work. Exams should help to shape your study, but they must never dominate it.

Remember—exams are the means to an end, not ends in themselves.

When should you enter an exam?

If you're not sure whether to enter for an exam, ask yourself the following questions. Be honest, and if you answer 'yes' to each one then you're probably ready.

1. Firstly (and most importantly), do you *want* to take the exam? It's a lot of hard work, and it simply won't get done if you're not really interested and enthusiastic.
2. Are you prepared to learn your scales and arpeggios?
3. Is your aural ability equal to the requirements of the grade you're thinking of taking?
4. Is your sight-reading ability up to the standard of your chosen grade?

Exams test your *overall musical ability*—don't enter if playing the pieces is the only thing that really interests you!

2. Preparation

Always allow sufficient time for your exam preparation. This will vary quite a lot from one person to another; experience and your teacher's advice will help you to decide how much time you should need. But be careful not to spend too long, in case you get bored and your pieces become stale.

Ideally, you should be just above the standard of the grade you decide to take. If you're really struggling with the material, then you're probably not ready for that grade yet. Remember too that it is a good idea to include pieces outside the exam syllabus during your preparation. Try to avoid playing the same pieces for weeks (sometimes even months) on end: it's like eating the same food day after day—rather boring, and certainly not particularly nourishing!

If you can, get involved in other musical activities: ensemble or orchestral playing, for example, choral singing or accompanying your friends. The more music you play, the better all-round musician you'll become, and the better your chances of doing well in an exam.

Finally, make sure that you check the syllabus very carefully, as exam requirements change from time to time. And don't forget to read the small print!

3. Practice

You've probably heard the expression 'Practice makes perfect'. If we add a word to make it 'Perfect practice makes perfect' we will have pin-pointed one of the most important keys to success.

If you can get into the habit of practising really carefully, thoughtfully, and methodically you'll be surprised just how much progress you're capable of making—and also how quickly you can make it.

Read this section often, until 'perfect practice' becomes a habit.

Regular practice is essential. It is NOT a good idea to limit your practice to one long session the evening before your lesson. You should practise for at least half an hour each day (more for the higher grades) to give your technique and musical imagination the opportunity to develop properly. Also, by working on a regular basis you'll find that as you work out and overcome each problem you'll enjoy your practice more. You really will feel yourself improving, and it will certainly please your teacher too!

Organize your practice so that you begin with warming-up exercises and then continue with some scales and arpeggios, a study (if you have one), pieces, and some sight-reading. Make out a daily check-list if you think it will encourage you to work more methodically.

	Sun.	Mon.	Tue.	Wed.	Thur.	Fri.	Sat.
Scales and arpeggios							
Pieces							
Study							
Sight-reading							

Try to devote more time to your weaker areas, rather than spending longer on those you particularly enjoy or are best at.

How to get the most from your practice

If you try to observe the following 'rules' you will very quickly begin to enjoy the fruits of a good practice technique.

Always be relaxed, patient, and methodical when you practise—impatience will make you frustrated and do you more harm than good. If you are not in the mood to practise, then don't! Try to avoid practising if you are tired; for really successful practice you must be both mentally and physically alert.

If you make a mistake, correct it at once. If you don't, you'll be surprised how quickly the mistake can become part of your performance and then it becomes twice as difficult to put right. (Remember that this doesn't apply when you're actually performing or sight-reading.)

Always listen *carefully* and *critically* to what you are playing. As you practise, try to think what your teacher might say to you—and act on it accordingly! If you have a tape recorder available, try recording your performances occasionally; this can be very revealing.

Spend most of your time practising sections or passages that you find particularly difficult. Practise them slowly at first until you have really mastered them, and then begin to increase the tempo. When you come to practise the same section at your next session, you may well find that it has still not improved as much as you would have liked. But don't be disheartened—begin again with slow practice, and in time you will succeed.

Practise the joins between sections very carefully: these are often the places where performances break down.

Use a metronome frequently.

Occasionally try to memorize a short phrase or passage (or even a whole piece)—play it with your eyes closed if you can, and listen. You should be able to concentrate fully on quality of sound, dynamic levels, phrasing, and musical shape. Pianists will often learn pieces from memory, but no one is actually *expected* to play from memory at their exam.

> There is a very good saying about practice:
>
> Amateurs practise until they get it right; professionals practise until it can't go wrong.
>
> *Practise like a professional!*

A practice check-list

Check each of these points every time you practise. Try to reach the stage where you do so automatically—when you do, you'll be practising really efficiently!

KEYBOARD PLAYERS

- Is your posture correct? Remember to check that (*a*) you're sitting properly at the keyboard, and (*b*) your hand shape and position are correct.
- Are you using the correct fingering?

- Are you using the pedal to gain the best effect? (It is often over-used!)
- Are you phrasing as marked?
- Are you giving character to your pieces?
- Is the rhythm correct? Don't forget the benefits of occasional practice with a metronome.
- Are you observing dynamic levels and other markings? Are there any markings you don't fully understand? If so, look them up and ask your teacher to explain them.
- Are you listening carefully and critically to everything you play?
- Remember to include some scales, some technical exercises, some studies and pieces, and some sight-reading in your practice.

STRING PLAYERS

- Is your posture correct? Take care that you're holding your instrument and bow correctly.
- Always check the position of the left wrist, which is so often held incorrectly.
- Have you tuned the strings carefully? Never practise on an out-of-tune instrument.
- Is your bow sufficiently rosined?
- Are you using the most efficient fingering?
- Is your intonation accurate?
- Are you listening carefully and critically to everything you play?
- Are you bowing as marked?
- Is the rhythm correct? Don't forget the benefits of occasional practice with a metronome.
- Are you phrasing musically?
- Are you giving character to your pieces?
- Are you observing dynamic levels and other markings? Are there any markings you don't fully understand? If so, look them up and ask your teacher to explain them.
- Remember to include some scales, some technical exercises, some studies and pieces, and some sight-reading in your practice.

WOODWIND AND BRASS PLAYERS

- Take care that you're holding your instrument correctly; check your posture and the position of your hands and fingers.
- Is the tone quality the best that you're capable of?
- Are you articulating (tonguing) as marked?
- Are you phrasing clearly and as marked?
- Is the rhythm correct? Don't forget the benefits of occasional practice with a metronome.
- Is your intonation accurate?
- Have you worked out the best places to breathe? It's a good idea to mark these and strictly observe them. Knowing when you are going to breathe should become part of your performance, and it will help you avoid unnecessary tension and the possibility of running out of breath in the middle of a phrase.
- Are you giving character to your pieces?
- Are you observing dynamic levels and other markings? Are there any markings you don't fully understand? If so, look them up and ask your teacher to explain them.
- Are you listening carefully and critically to everything you play?
- Remember to include some scales, some technical exercises, some studies and pieces, and some sight-reading in your practice.

PERCUSSIONISTS

- Is your posture correct? Are you holding the sticks correctly?
- Is the rhythm correct? Don't forget the benefits of occasional practice with a metronome.
- Are you observing dynamic levels and other markings? Are there any markings you don't fully understand? If so, look them up and ask your teacher to explain them.
- Are you playing with an evenly controlled sound?
- Remember to include some scales (where appropriate), some technical exercises (rudiments), some studies and pieces, and some sight-reading in your practice.

SINGERS

- Use a mirror (as large as possible) to make sure that you look natural and are not developing any mannerisms (such as lifting an arm or making faces).
- Is your diction clear? For songs in English, try singing them to a friend; they'll soon tell you whether they can understand the words!
- For songs in a foreign language, be sure that your pronunciation is as authentic as possible. Ensure that you know the meaning of the text so that you can capture its mood.
- Is the rhythm correct? Don't forget the benefits of occasional practice with a metronome.
- Are you observing dynamic levels and other markings? Are there any markings you don't fully understand? If so, look them up and ask your teacher to explain them.
- Are you singing in tune? Occasionally test your intonation by comparing your pitch with the same notes on a well-tuned piano.
- Are you listening critically to everything you sing?
- Remember to include some scales, some technical exercises, some pieces, and some sight-reading in your practice.

4. Scales and arpeggios

Scales and arpeggios often seem like giant hurdles in your exam preparation. If you work at them methodically and thoughtfully, and understand their great importance in improving all aspects of your playing, they will become both more enjoyable to learn and more meaningful to practise.

Really knowing your scales and arpeggios will:
- vastly improve all aspects of your technique
- improve the speed at which you learn new pieces, since many difficult passages are really only scale and arpeggio patterns in disguise
- improve your ability to sight-read, because they form the melodic shapes on which much music is based
- earn you more marks in exams.

The problems, and how to overcome them

1. Playing your scales and arpeggios from memory

First of all, you must *know* the key signature and therefore the notes of each scale and arpeggio. Never 'feel your way' through a scale—you'll almost always make mistakes and play unrhythmically. If you have trouble remembering the notes, try the following method.

(a) With the key signature in mind, *say* the names of the notes out loud. Don't *play* the scale or arpeggio until you can say the notes confidently and correctly. You should now be in a position where you know the notes you're going to play.

(b) Pianists: play very slowly, still actually saying the note-names out loud as you play. Instrumentalists: finger the notes without sounding them, saying the note-names as you do so.

(c) Finally, play the scale or arpeggio slowly, *thinking* the note-names.

The extra time this method will take is well worth the effort—you really will begin to *know* your scales.

NEVER play by ear. If you're one of those musicians whose excuse for playing wrong notes is 'Well, I usually get it right the second or third time,' then you *don't know* that scale or arpegggio!

2. Developing fluency and control

Scales and arpeggios must sound fluent, and must be played with a steady and even rhythmic shape. To help develop these qualities, practise scales and arpeggios using varying rhythms, for example those shown below.

Scales   Arpeggios

Similarly, use differing articulation patterns such as the following:

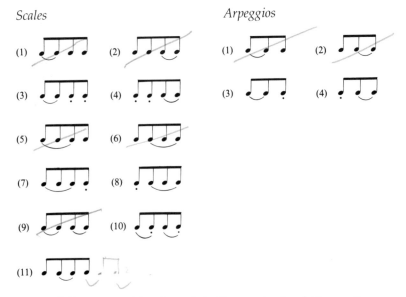

Scales

(1) (2) (3) (4) (5) (6) (7) (8) (9) (10) (11)

Arpeggios

(1) (2) (3) (4)

Use a different combination of rhythm and articulation patterns each time you practise, perhaps rhythm pattern no. 2 with articulation pattern no. 4, for example. This has the advantage of adding variety to your scales and arpeggios, whilst at the same time concentrating the mind.

Practise with a metronome. Begin with it at a slow setting and gradually increase the speed. Make a note of your fastest tempo at each session (but never play faster than your technique will allow).

3. Intonation

For all non-keyboard players, and particularly string players, intonation is very important. You must have a clear idea of the pitch of the next note before you play it. Very slow scale practice, trying to hear the next note in your head before you play it, will help develop this ability. Also practise by checking each note against the same notes on a well-tuned piano or electronic tuning device. Practising this with a friend can be fun, and will help you both to develop a better sense of accurate tuning.

4. Tone (sound) quality

Always remember to play scales and arpeggios with your best possible sound and with an even tone quality. Listen carefully and try to match the tone quality from one note to the next; very slow practice will help here. To enable you to gain more control, try using varying dynamic levels (everything from *ppp* to *fff*), sometimes including crescendos and diminuendos.

Here are a few examples, showing varying dynamics and different patterns of rhythm and articulation.

Performing scales and arpeggios

The following general remarks apply to everyone.

You should play your scales and arpeggios rhythmically and all at the same tempo (to be decided with your teacher). Don't play the scales you know well at twice the tempo of those you don't—this doesn't give a very good impression! The higher the grade, the greater the fluency required, but the tempo you choose must always be determined by the limits of your technique: playing at a slower tempo with absolute precision will impress the examiner much more than playing fast but without total control. Play them about *mf* and keep the tone or touch even throughout, taking care not to accent the top note or lose rhythmic control as you change direction. The movement of your fingers should always be firm, precise, and well directed. This will give an added confidence to your performance.

Make sure you have a list of all the required scales and arpeggios written down for easy reference. But don't always practise them in the same order: you can never predict how they will come in the exam. As it approaches, try to get someone to ask you to play a number of scales and arpeggios each time you practise—not necessarily in the order you have them written down.

Very occasionally you may have a mental block and completely forget a particular scale that you have been asked. Don't panic! Relax and concentrate your mind on the key note. For example, if you were trying to play F sharp minor, just think of F sharp and then think of the key signature. Begin the scale a little slower than usual, and it will almost certainly come back to you straight away.

The following remarks are divided into different groups to offer more particular advice, but there is no reason why you shouldn't read them all!

KEYBOARD PLAYERS

Take particular care that your hands are precisely co-ordinated, which means that your right and left hands must move absolutely together. Accenting groups of twos, threes, etc. is a good way to practise this. You must also play with an absolutely even rhythm; practising in different rhythms is an effective way to achieve this (see above).

STRING PLAYERS

Concentrate on a good bowing action as well as accurate intonation and good tone quality. Always take care to finger your scales very carefully. Guitarists: aim to play each note very cleanly; your finger action must therefore be carefully directed, and positioning on the fingerboard must be precise.

WOODWIND AND BRASS PLAYERS

In tongued/staccato scales, you should always play notes lightly and without accents, making sure that you give all the notes equal duration. This will help to make your scales sound neat and rhythmic. When playing arpeggios, pay particular attention to moving your fingers together when moving more than one finger at a time.

Remember that scales and arpeggios on woodwind and brass instruments must be played carefully in tune, but just fingering a note correctly doesn't necessarily guarantee accurate intonation. Be aware of the effect that alternative fingerings may have on intonation.

What is the examiner looking for?

■ Correct notes and rhythmic playing.
■ An even and carefully controlled touch or tone.
■ Accurate intonation.
■ A sense of musical line: remember that scales are music too, and your performance of each example should have shape and direction.

---

5. Studies

Before you begin work on a study you should look through it carefully and decide which particular technical problems are involved—that is, the *actual purpose* of it.

Practising studies

At first you should practise studies slowly, section by section, bar by bar, sometimes note by note. If there is a difficult passage, play it in several different rhythms, slowly initially and then gradually up to speed. Make sure you *really do* overcome each technical problem before moving on to the next: half-solved technical problems will always cause you to stumble, and will result in an uneven performance.

String players: make sure that you mark in all the bowing and fingering where necessary, and then stick to it. Naturally you must concentrate on playing well in tune. Always listen carefully to the sound you are making.

Woodwind and brass players: decide on breathing places in advance and mark these in the copy: mistakes are often made as a result of finding yourself out of breath or by worrying about where the next breath will be as you are playing. Knowing when to breathe and how much air to take in before each phrase is very much a part of your performance.

You *must* count—you'll never develop a really good rhythmic sense if you don't. The use of a metronome when practising studies is strongly recommended. Where there are particular rhythmic difficulties or complications, sub-divide the beat or basic pulse. For example, the passage that follows would more easily be counted in quavers than in crotchets.

François Garnier

Avoid making unnecessarily strong accents on beats, except for a slight feeling for the natural bar accents (first beat of the bar, or first and third in 4/4 time).

Don't tap your foot to keep time, though tapping your toe inside your shoe is acceptable if you have to, and certainly less visible and audible!

Performing studies

It is very important to play your study at a steady tempo throughout, keeping the rhythm accurate. Make sure that you observe all markings carefully. Dynamic levels should be carefully related to each other and to the style of the music. If no dynamic markings are provided, choose your own with the help of your teacher. Always aim to produce an even tone and the best quality of sound that you can.

What is the examiner looking for?

- An understanding of the purpose of the study; this should be clear to the examiner from your performance!
- An accurate performance: correct notes and rhythms.
- A steady pulse.
- Observance of all markings.
- A well-controlled and pleasing tone quality, and a *musical* performance with shape and direction.

---

6. Pieces

Where you have a choice of repertoire, learn as much of it as possible before making your final decision. With the help of your teacher, choose pieces that are well within your technical capabilities and if possible ones that are well contrasted.

Knowing your pieces

Initially you should practise pieces in the same way as studies (see the preceding section). Make sure that you're aware of all the technical problems, and deal with them in the same way as you would in a study. Practise particularly difficult sections until you can play them with ease, and make sure that each section moves smoothly into the next.

Check and learn the meaning of all the terms and markings used by the composer and make sure you are observing them musically. For example, a 'rallentando' in a Baroque movement will need to be interpreted differently from one in a piece from the Romantic period. As you can see, it's very important to find out when the composer lived and something about the main features of his period; this will help you to interpret his music and so give your performance a sense of style.

It is *particularly* important for you to understand the character and style of your chosen pieces. What is the mood of the piece you are learning? Is it happy or sad? What *kind* of happy or sad? Is it bold or gentle? What can you do to convey the necessary boldness or gentleness? Try to get to the heart of each piece and then work out how best to communicate its mood. Remember that a bland performance, a performance without expression, even if it is accurate, will rarely earn you particularly high marks at any grade.

Singers: how you look while singing is of great importance; no song will really *sound* happy unless you *look* happy.

Practising with an accompanist

Make sure that you plan sufficient rehearsal time with your accompanist. Nothing can be so off-putting to an instrumentalist as hearing the piano accompaniment for the first time five minutes before the exam! Do make sure that your accompanist will be able to play the piano part: sometimes these are difficult, and an accompanist who is struggling can spoil an otherwise well-prepared performance.

The better you know the piano parts, the more able you will be to give a convincing performance. Take particular care that you know where to come in if there are rests, or solo sections for the accompanist.

What is the examiner looking for?

■ The right notes, well-controlled rhythm, and a steady pulse.
■ Observance of dynamic levels, phrasing, and other character markings.
■ Intonation.
■ Most important, whatever the grade, is that the examiner feels you understand the music and are really trying to communicate its *character.*

---

7. Sight-reading

How to tackle sight-reading

There are two golden rules which you must remember:

COUNT (which will help you to get the rhythm right).
DON'T STOP once you have begun.

You will probably be given a short time to look at the piece before you are asked to play. If you use this time carefully, you can learn a lot. You'll be surprised just how much you can notice in say 30 seconds!

Try to pick out the following:

- *Time signature.* This will probably tell you what to count, though if there is a lot of quaver and semiquaver movement, you may decide to count in subdivisions of the beat.
- *Key signature.* Look through the piece and notice at least the first note affected by the key signature.
- *Tempo and stylistic indications.* Both those given at the beginning, and any later in the piece.
- *Dynamic markings.* Don't be too timid about these—make clear contrasts between levels if possible.
- *Phrasing and articulation markings.*
- *Bowings.*
- *Rests.*
- *Accidentals.* Watch out for the slightly more unusual ones like A♯, E♯, G♭, F♭, etc. if they occur.
- *Unusual rhythms* that may cause particular problems.
- *Clef changes.* Pianists: watch out for the use of the treble clef in the left-hand part. Cellists, bassoonists, and trombonists: you may be expected to read in a variety of clefs. Note these before you begin and make sure that you have had enough practice reading in these clefs to feel confident.

To help you to improve this quick detection of important points, try playing the following game with your teacher or a friend. Practise looking at a piece for about 30 seconds, and then get your teacher or friend to ask you questions on the various points above. Try to answer from memory. Do this regularly and you'll soon learn to notice all you need.

Performing the sight-reading test

Count yourself in with at least one bar in your chosen tempo and continue to count throughout the piece. ALWAYS KEEP GOING. Try to look ahead while you're playing, and if you make a mistake, ignore it—don't ever stop to put it right!

As you are playing, glance at the key signature (if there is one) at the beginning of each new line to remind yourself of the particular sharps or flats. Remember that accidentals maintain their effect throughout a bar.

Remember also that most music is written in a particular key and often very much based on scale and arpeggio patterns.

Spotting these patterns through knowing your scales and arpeggios thoroughly will help to develop real fluency in your sight-reading.

Always sight-read musically and with your best tone quality.

What is the examiner looking for?

- Accurate notes and rhythm.
- Observance of markings.
- Musical phrasing.
- Perhaps most importantly: a performance that maintains a *steady tempo* without any hesitations (even if it means a wrong note or two!).

---

8. Aural

The purpose of aural training is to encourage you to *listen* carefully and musically. Practise aural regularly; two or three sessions just before the exam is not enough. The idea that some people can 'do' aural and some people just can't is really quite untrue: your aural ability *will* improve with regular practice.

At the exam

Listen to the examiner's instructions before each test; it's quite acceptable to ask for an instruction to be repeated if you didn't hear clearly or are not quite sure what you are required to do.

Be confident and try to give spontaneous responses. An alert and musical answer may often impress the examiner even though it might not be completely accurate.

For tests that require singing, remember that it's not the *quality* of your voice that's being tested. For those with breaking voices, whistling or humming are acceptable.

The following sections cover most of the standard tests. There are of course many other methods you may like to try—be guided by your teacher. Some of the sections include 'practical tips'. These are suggestions either for relating the aural tests to your instrumental playing or for extending the tests to develop your musicianship further. Try them during your lesson or perhaps with a friend: they're not part of the exam material, but will help make your aural practice more interesting.

Singing back melodies

Aim to sing both melody and rhythm accurately, holding long notes for their full value. Don't panic if the melody seems endless: relax and try to sing back as accurate an answer as possible, making sure you have at least the same number of beats and bars. It is better to invent a convincing ending (you never know—it may be correct!) than to come to a hesitant and embarrassed silence two thirds of the way through. Avoid singing with the tune when it is played a second time—it's much better just to listen carefully and there will be much more chance of getting it right.

Practical tip

Occasionally try playing back the melody on your instrument. By actually having to *play* the notes, this exercise will encourage you to really listen to the melodic shape and its intervals. Before attempting longer phrases, begin by trying to play back just short two- or three-note patterns.

Clapping rhythms

Try two fingers held together tapping onto the palm of the other hand; this requires less physical effort than clapping, making more complicated groupings easier. As in the melodic tests, if the examples seem very long and you're not absolutely sure of the answer, try at least to give a good approximation with the same number of beats or bars.

> Practical tip
>
> Try tapping the beat with your toe and the actual rhythm with your hands. This will give you a clearer idea of how the rhythm fits into the beat.

Identifying and beating time

Listen for the strong beats, which usually indicate the first beat of the bar. Remember that all beats are of the same length.

Keep your beat reasonably small and clear when beating time. The following shapes should be used:

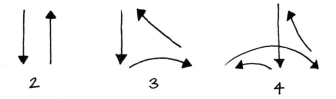

2   3   4

> Practical tip
>
> Occasionally try to work out the time signature when you're listening to music. Beat time to records or tapes (probably best done in the privacy of your bedroom!).

Describing the time values

If there are any complex groupings, sub-divide the beat; you may like to think of a quaver pulse in 3/4, or a semiquaver pulse in 6/8.

For example, imagine that the rhythm was

Silently tapping a quaver pulse while you *think* the rhythm may well help make it much clearer to you.

THINK

TAP

> **Practical tip**
>
> On a piece of manuscript paper try to work out and write down the rhythms of tunes you know. Ask your teacher or a friend to try to recognize the tune from its rhythm alone.

Intervals

Try to hear the interval in your head: avoid audibly 'singing up' the interval if possible. It may be helpful to attach a well-known tune to an interval. For example, the interval of a perfect fourth forms the opening two notes of 'Away in a manger'. Sing the notes in your head. Recognizing intervals in this way is a good step towards really knowing them, and you can build up your own personal list of tunes for each interval.

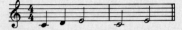
Recognizing major or minor

Major = happy and *minor = sad* usually works!

Recognizing the position of triads

Root position. Listen to the interval formed by the lowest and highest notes; a perfect fifth indicates a root-position chord.

First inversion. The lowest and highest notes form a sixth, with the larger interval between the top two of the three notes.

Second inversion. Again, the outer notes form a sixth but the larger interval is now between the bottom two notes.

Cadences

Listen to the bass notes at the cadence.

In a *perfect* cadence the bass moves from V to I, with a strong feeling of finality—the musical equivalent of a full stop!

In a *plagal* cadence the bass moves from IV to I. Many hymns end this way with an 'Amen', and you can recognize the 'feel' of a plagal cadence from this.

In an *interrupted* cadence there's an element of surprise, as the bass moves from V to VI, rather than from V to I.

In an *imperfect* cadence the bass note moves to V and rests there. You should be able to feel the music wanting to move on, perhaps eventually back to I. If the perfect cadence is a musical full stop, the imperfect cadence is like a musical comma.

> Practical tip
> Try to identify cadences in the pieces you are playing.

Recognizing chords

As in cadences, listen carefully to the bass notes. Remember that in a major example, chord VI will be minor, and in a minor example, chords V and VI will be major.

Modulations

Register carefully in which mode (major or minor) the example begins. A modulation from major to minor or minor to major should cause no problems. A modulation to the dominant adds a sharp or removes a flat, and so a 'sharpening' or 'brightening' effect may be felt. The sub-dominant adds a flat or removes a sharp, and thus a 'flattening' effect may be detected.

9. Viva voce

Some examination boards include a *viva voce*. This is where you will be asked questions on particular aspects of the notation, structure, or general background of the pieces you are playing. Some knowledge of the structure of the work, and the composer's historical background and style is important and may well help you in giving a characterful and more stylish performance. So whether or not you have a *viva voce*, knowing the following can do you no harm:

- the meaning of all notation symbols, markings, and foreign terms
- the value of notes and rests
- the meaning of time signatures and rhythms
- the pitch-name of any note
- the meaning of key signatures and accidentals
- the names and interpretations of ornaments
- something of the composer and his historical background.

10. Instruments

Take pride in the condition of your instrument—look after it, keep it clean, and make sure that you have it serviced occasionally, particularly in the case of woodwind instruments.

KEYBOARD PLAYERS

Pianists: try to have at least one practice session on a grand piano before the exam, particularly if you don't usually practice on one: the 'feel' may be different from an upright. To have to play a grand piano for the first time at the exam can be a rather daunting experience. If at all possible, see if you can have a practice on the piano that will be used in the actual exam.

Organists: make sure that you have practised on the exam instrument to become familiar with the layout of stops, and the touch of both manuals and pedals.

STRING PLAYERS

Always keep a spare set of strings in case of accidents. Check that you have a good mute if necessary, and that you have your rosin.

WOODWIND AND BRASS PLAYERS

Make sure, with the help of your teacher, that your instrument is in full working order. A check-up with a qualified instrument repairer or technician a few weeks before the exam is a very good idea and is really essential before taking one of the higher grades.

Oboists: try to persuade your teacher to be nearby on the day of the exam if at all possible. These instruments are notorious for developing an ailment at the worst possible moment.

Where appropriate, have at least one or two tried and tested spare reeds at the ready.

Check that the valves and tuning slides on brass instruments are well oiled, and that the joints on wind instruments are adequately greased, enabling you to carry out any tuning adjustments with ease.

PERCUSSIONISTS

Check that the snares on the snare drum are working efficiently. Make sure that you're familiar with the particular tuning mechanism of the timpani you'll be using in the exam.

11. Mock exams

Ask your teacher for a mock exam about three weeks before the real one. This will give you the important experience of actually practising 'the exam' and it should allow you enough time to put things right, if necessary. Your teacher should try to make the exam similar in as many details as possible to the real thing, marking your performance too if you like. One or two more 'mocks' before the exam would be a good idea, perhaps with different people 'examining' if you can find anyone willing! You may well find that taking these mocks will help to reduce any worries or nerves that you may have.

12. On the day

If you have worked carefully and methodically in the weeks preceding the examination, if you have thoroughly learnt your pieces, mastered your scales and arpeggios, and have your sight-reading and aural well prepared, you should be feeling both confident and ready to make a good impression on the examiner!

Make sure that you've had a good night's sleep. Dress neatly and comfortably, and check that you have your music (including piano accompaniments where necessary) before leaving home. Guitarists: remember your footstool if you use one.

Ensure that your instrument and hands are clean.

Arrive at least ten minutes before the examination. Don't hurry, but try to relax: you'll feel much happier.

Nerves

Whether you like it or not, nerves and exams go together. Don't worry about being nervous—without nerves you wouldn't feel the necessary excitement and sense of occasion, and they actually help produce the extra energy you need.

You can learn to control them, though. If you are particularly nervous, sit quietly for a few minutes taking slow, deep breaths, breathing out slowly through the mouth. This will help to slow down your heartbeat and help you to feel more relaxed. If your hands or arms are shaking, drop them by your sides and try to feel their weight in your fingertips. In the exam room, a slight alteration to the height of the music stand or piano stool, or even adjusting the music on the stand, may help to calm you.

Remember also, that examiners *are* human!

All performers, however experienced, are at least a little nervous before a performance. If you are sufficiently well prepared, and have had at least one mock exam and perhaps performed your pieces at a concert or to family or friends, there should be very little reason for anything but the smallest degree of nerves. Just concentrate your mind on doing your best and enjoying your playing.

In the waiting room

KEYBOARD PLAYERS
Keep your fingers warm and flexible. Cold fingers just won't work properly!

STRING PLAYERS
Tune your instrument carefully so that once in the exam room you'll only have to make minor adjustments. Bows should be carefully rosined. If you have recently been practising, check that the instrument is clear of excess rosin. Make sure you keep your fingers warm.

WOODWIND AND BRASS PLAYERS
Be sure that your instrument is adequately warmed up before entering the exam room. If you're not actually able to play (if the exam and waiting rooms are too close to each other, for example), then blow gently and silently through the instrument. Make sure that you keep your fingers warm.

Woodwind players in particular should check that the tone holes are free from water (especially if you have been practising for any length of time immediately before the exam). If your instrument does begin to misbehave during the exam, wait for an appropriate moment and then blow the water out of the hole. If certain notes really refuse to sound at all, then stop and take whatever steps are necessary. Most examiners will understand. Brass players: blow out any water before you begin, or between pieces when you need to.

SINGERS
Hum quietly!

PERCUSSIONISTS
You may like to practise quietly on a practice pad.

The moment of truth

Try to remain relaxed. Enter and leave the exam room without hurrying. A smile will often help.

Be sure to know the titles and composers of your pieces (and how to pronounce them!); the examiner will probably ask you what you are going to play at the beginning of the exam.

If you have an instrument that requires tuning, take your time and tune carefully. Don't forget that for the higher grades most examination boards require you to tune your instrument unaided, so make sure that you're well used to doing this. Re-tune between movements and pieces if you need to, and do take your time. Wind and brass players: avoid using vibrato when tuning.

Before you begin, stand or sit still for a moment and think about the character of the music you are about to play. Get into the habit of doing this when you are practising. It will help you to concentrate, calm your nerves, and help to make the opening of the piece confident and musical.

If you have an accompanist and there is no piano introduction, co-ordinate the start of the piece by a small movement of your instrument. Usually this will be one or two beats in the time of the piece. This should be well rehearsed, so that it looks professional and will help to shape your performance.

Don't show any signs of annoyance if you make a mistake—just continue playing as if nothing had happened. Never comment verbally on errors (even a 'tut' should be avoided!). Even the best players will make the odd mistake during a performance, and the secret is to ignore it completely rather than drawing attention to it or letting it disturb your concentration.

43

Pianists, string players, and guitarists should avoid pulling faces and breathing noisily; this is usually distracting and certainly does not add to a performance.

Instrumentalists and singers should remain still during rests. Concentrate on counting and on your next entry. If there are a few bars for the accompanist alone at the end of the piece, don't heave a sigh of relief or relax the moment *you* have stopped playing. Remain absolutely still for a few moments after each piece. Remember that you are performing and that a performance begins *before* the piece and ends *after* it is finished. This will add to the overall impression.

Instrumentalists who have to put their instruments down during the exam (during the aural for example) should take care, particularly if it's an instrument with a reed.

Percussionists, check that the snares are off when (and if) you're playing the timpani.

13. After the exam

After the exam, *don't* begin working on the next grade straight away. Learn some new repertoire, perhaps some other pieces on the syllabus from the grade you've just taken. Don't forget the scales you have learnt: not only will they come around again in future exams, but they're always essential for keeping your technique up to scratch. After a suitable period of time you can begin preparing for your next exam.

The result

If you were well prepared and you played musically and confidently, with scales, aural, and sight-reading all going without major mishaps, then you should pass—and pass well.

Occasionally things just don't go so well for one reason or another. If you should fail (and you feel you *were* prepared), then you must put it behind you and get on with your playing—it doesn't actually matter that much. Whether you take that grade again or begin to move on to the next is a matter for you to discuss with your teacher, but whatever you do, try not to let it upset you unduly.

14. A final thought

Music is an art. Music exams are to help in motivating you to become more proficient in expressing this art. Commitment, involvement, and the desire to do well should ensure success.

Personal information & addresses

Name: _____

Instrument: _____

_____
Teacher:

_____
Tel:

Music Shop:

_____
Tel:

Piano Tuner:

_____
Tel:

Instrument Shop:

_____
Tel:

Instrument repairer:

_____
Tel: